PRESENTED BY

The Neergaards
in memory of
Elizabeth Brown.
Rogers Albright

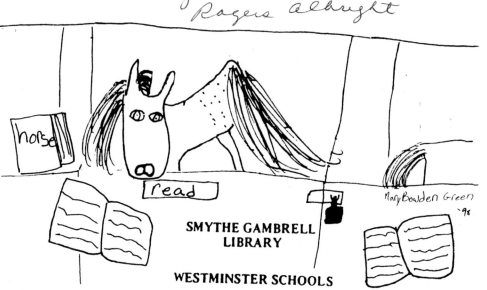

horse

read

MaryBowden Green
'98

**SMYTHE GAMBRELL
LIBRARY**

WESTMINSTER SCHOOLS

LLAMAS

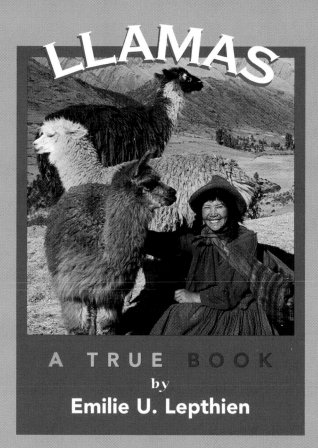

A TRUE BOOK

by

Emilie U. Lepthien

Children's Press®
A Division of Grolier Publishing
New York London Hong Kong Sydney
Danbury, Connecticut

To the Norris
grandchildren

Reading Consultant
Linda Cornwell
Learning Resource Consultant
Indiana Department of
Education

A Peruvian girl and her
baby llama

Library of Congress Cataloging-in-Publication Data

Lepthien, Emilie U. (Emilie Utteg)
    Llamas / by Emilie U. Lepthien.
        p.   cm. — (A True book)
    Includes bibliographical references (p.   ) and index.
    Summary: Describes the physical characteristics and habits of
llamas and their relatives, and the ways they have been used
throughout history, particularly by the Incas.
    ISBN 0-516-20160-3 (lib.bdg.)   ISBN 0-516-26108-8 (pbk.)
    1. Llamas—Juvenile literature. [1. Llamas.] I. Title. II. Series.
QL737.U54L46 1996
599.73′6—dc20   96-1392
                                                                    CIP
                                                                    AC

Contents

Llamas Long Ago

When the Inca people arrived in Peru in the A.D. 1110s, they found a strange animal that earlier people had domesticated. These long-haired animals looked something like small camels without humps. They were llamas—members of the camel family.

For more than 4,000 years, the earlier people of Peru had kept herds of llamas. They used them as pack animals in the high Andes mountains.

The Inca people came to depend on these gentle, sturdy animals as well. The llamas carried building materials for roads, temples, and the vast irrigation systems of the Inca Empire. They brought gold and silver ore from the mines to be

A llama standing in front of ancient Inca ruins that were built with the help of llamas

smelted and made into beautiful treasures.

By the 1400s, when Spanish settlers arrived in South America, llamas were very important to the people of the Andes. Llama wool was used to make clothing, and llama hide was used to make shoes. The people also depended on the llama for food.

A piece of ancient Peruvian cloth wove from llama wool

Many Peruvian Indians still wear clothing made from llama wool.

Llamas Today

Llamas are still used as pack animals by the Indians living in the Andes mountains in Peru, Bolivia, Ecuador, Chile, and Argentina. The largest numbers of llamas live in Peru.

There are four related species of animals known collectively as *lamoids.* The llama and the

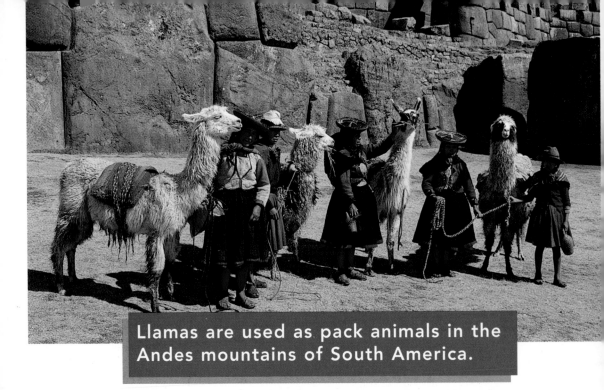
Llamas are used as pack animals in the Andes mountains of South America.

alpaca are domesticated. The guanaco and the vicuna are wild. Llamas are the largest and strongest of the four species.

Llamas, alpacas, and guanacos live in the Andes at altitudes of 12,000 to 14,000 feet (3,658 to 4,267 meters). Vicunas like to feed higher up in the mountains—at heights of 16,000 to 18,000 feet (4,876 to 5,486 m). That's more than three miles above sea level!

Young alpacas

A female llama and her baby

Llamas with Big Hearts

Llamas that live high up in the Andes mountains have adapted to their environment. They have enlarged hearts and lungs. There is less oxygen in the air at higher altitudes, so bigger hearts and lungs help these llamas get the oxygen they need to survive.

Guanacos in the Andes Mountains of Chile (left) and vicunas in Peru (right)

Llamas weigh 250 to 450 pounds (113 to 203 kilograms) and stand about 4 feet (120 centimeters) high at the shoulder. They have long necks and small heads.

Some llamas are a solid color—white, brown, or black. Calico llamas have patches of white, brown, and black hairs.

Pack Animals

High in the Andes today, male llamas are still used as pack animals. They are never sheared. Under their thick, heavy outer coat is a layer of soft down that keeps them warm. Female llamas are never used as pack animals.

A llama does not need a saddle or blanket under its pack. The coarse hair of its heavy outer coat protects it.

A llama can carry a load of up to 100 pounds (45 kg) in

costals—pack bags woven from llama wool. The bags are slung across the animal's back with an equal weight on each side. The costals are tied on with *sogas*, ropes also made from llama wool.

Llamas are strong and sure-footed. But if a llama feels that the load is too heavy—or thinks it has worked hard enough—it kneels down and refuses to budge.

Soft Feet

Llamas are very sure-footed on trails. This is one reason why they make such good pack animals in the rocky Andes mountains.

Llamas do not have hooves. That's why they do not disturb the ground on the trail as much as hoofed animals like horses or mules would. A llama's feet are cloven, or divided. Each foot has two toes and is padded on the bottom.

In the Andes, a llama's toenails wear down from walking on gravel and stones. Llamas living on farms or ranches in North America must have their toenails clipped or they would grow too long.

Llamas have an interesting gait, or walk. When llamas walk, they move both feet on

Llamas are very sure-footed, even on steep trails.

Llama feet are padded on the bottom

the same side of the body at the same time. When they run, their legs move like a horse— the left front leg moving with the right hind leg.

Vicunas eating

Feeding

In the *altiplano*—the high plains between the mountains—llamas, alpacas, and guanacos browse on grasses, shrubs, and small trees. Vicunas, which live at higher altitudes, feed on moss and lichens.

Llamas need fresh fluids daily. However, they can go

Llamas don't need to drink a lot of water because they get their fluids from the plants they eat.

without eating for several days. They do not need to drink much water. They get most of their fluids from the moisture in the plants they eat.

Llamas have no upper front teeth. But their gums are very

hard, and their lips are very flexible. They grasp grasses or leaves with their lips, and press the leaves against their gums. Then they crop off the food with their sharp lower front teeth. They use their flat back teeth to chew their food.

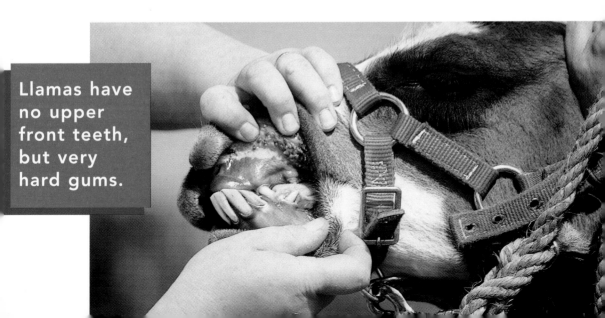

Llamas have no upper front teeth, but very hard gums.

Cud Chewers

Mammals that have four stomachs, chew their cud, and have cloven hooves are classified as *ruminants*. Cattle, sheep, goats, bison, deer, antelopes, and giraffes are ruminants. Llamas, which have three stomachs, are modified ruminants. Llamas

A llama chewing its cud

and other ruminants are *herbivores*. This means that they feed on plant materials. Llamas, like other ruminants, are cud chewers. They chew their food quickly and swallow it. In the first stomach, the food is partially digested. Then the food is brought back up into the llama's mouth to be chewed again and swallowed. This regurgitated food is called cud. Llamas chew their cud at night.

After the cud is swallowed again, it goes through the second and third stomachs, where it is completely digested.

Crias

Baby llamas are called *crias.*
They are born one at a time.
A cria is born 11½ months

A mother llama and her newborn cria

after a male and female llama have mated. In the Andes, they are born early in the day, when the sun is warm. The mother llama nurses the baby for five to six months. After that, the young llama takes care of itself.

A cria nursing

A young llama and its mother

Some llamas like the company of other animals.

Llamas like to live in small herds.

Social Animals

Llamas like company. They prefer living in small herds. A single llama is content if it has a dog or sheep as company.

Llamas use their long ears to communicate with others. They can turn their ears in different directions.

A llama's ears may show that a llama is curious (left), relaxed (center), or afraid (right).

When they are curious, their ears stand up. When they are relaxed, their ears lie back. When they are frightened, their ears lie close to their necks.

Llamas have another way to express themselves. When

they are very angry or scared, llamas may spit. Usually, they spit at each other, but they have been known to spit at people, too.

A llama spitting

Llamas also communicate by making sounds. They hum! Their humming sounds something like a cat's purr. South American people call this sound "praying."

Llamas usually hum when they are contented. But if the hum sounds like whining, it may mean that the llama is alarmed.

A female llama who is separated from her baby makes a noise that sounds

Llamas often communicate by making noises.

like a bicycle horn. A male llama may snort like a horse when it sees a female. Females respond with short clicking sounds.

The Other Lamoids

Vicunas, the smallest of the lamoids, are only two and a half feet high at the shoulder. They weigh from 75 to 100 pounds (34 to 45 kg). Vicuna females, their cria, and one male form a small herd.

Like all lamoids, vicunas have two layers of wool. The

Vicunas

top layer is coarse. The down
undercoat is the softest of any
lamoid. The fine reddish wool
of vicunas is highly prized.

Guanacos are very timid.
They are as tall as llamas, but
they weigh less. In southern

South America, guanacos were the main source of meat and hides for many years. Guanaco wool is coarse, but it once made warm clothing for Inca peasants. Now

Guanacos

An unsheared alpaca

guanacos have decreased in numbers. They are in need of protection as their grazing lands are used by domestic herds of cattle and sheep.

Alpacas are smaller than llamas. Their necks are shorter, and they are not strong enough to work as pack animals.

Alpacas in South America are sheared when they are two years old. Shearing does not hurt them. For seven years, each animal produces six pounds (three kg) of wool at a shearing. Most of the wool is brown or black, but some alpacas produce white or multicolored wool. White wool brings the highest price.

An alpaca being sheared

Useful Alpaca Wool

Many people in the Andes mountains wear beautiful handmade clothing made of **alpaca wool**. After the wool is **sheared** from the alpaca's body, it is **spun** into yarn (top left). The yarn is then **dyed**, and **woven** into fabric on a loom (top right). The result is a colorful, warm piece of clothing such as this hat (bottom).

Llamas in North America

About 100 years ago, the first llamas were brought to the United States. Now llamas are raised for their wool in almost every state and in Canada.

Sometimes rangers use llamas to patrol areas where they cannot use a car or truck. Many people hire llamas as

Llamas on a trail in Colorado

pack animals on treks through the Rocky Mountains.

For many years, llamas were raised as a hobby in North America. Today, more and more uses are being found for these gentle creatures. They are becoming increasingly popular.

To Find Out More

Here are some additional resources to help you learn more about llamas:

Organizations

Smithsonian: National Zoological Park
3000 Block of
Connecticut Avenue, NW
Washington, DC 20008
202-673-4800
http://www.si.sgi.com/per-spect.afafam/afazoo.htm

American Zoo and Aquarium Association
7970-D Old Georgetown Rd.
Bethesda, MD 20814-2493
301-907-7777
301-907-2890 (fax)

International Llama Association
2755 S. Locust Street, #114
Denver, CO 80222
1-800-WHY-LAMA
intlllama@aol.com

Llama Association of North America
1800 S. Obenchain Road
Eagle Point, OR 97524-9437
Llamainfo@aol.com

Sierra Club
730 Polk Street
San Francisco, CA 94109
415-776-2211
415-776-0350 (fax)
http://www.sierraclub.org/

Books

Arnold, Caroline, **Llama.**
Morrow Junior Books,
1988.

Conklin, Gladys, **Llamas of
South America.**
Holiday House, 1975.

LaBonte, Gail, **The Llama.**
Dillon Press, Inc, 1989.

Online Sites

Electronic Zoo
*http//www.zi.biologie.uni-
muenchen.de/~st2042/
exotic.html*

Llama Fact Sheet
*http://www.nbn.com/
people/camelid/Llama
FAQ.html*

Llama Web
*http:/ww.llamaweb.com/
degraham/*

**Llight Up Your Life
with Llamas**
*http://www.bestweb.com/
star/haven/llama.html*

**National Parks
Electronic Bookstore**
http://mesaverde.org/
npeb/books/10307240584.
html

Important Words

adapt to adjust to new conditions

crop to cut off

domesticate to tame a wild animal or plant

down fine, soft hair

enlarge to make or become bigger

environment a person or animal's natural surroundings

irrigation the process of bringing water to land where crops are grown

lichens mosslike plants that grow in patches on rocks or trees

pack animals an animal used to carry a pack or bundle

regurgitate to bring up partially digested food

shear to cut the hair or fleece from

smelt to melt ore in a furnace in order to obtain metal

Index

M eet the Author

Emilie U. Lepthien received her B.A. and M.S. degrees from Northwestern University. She taught upper-grade science and social studies and was a school principal in Chicago, Illinois for twenty years.